THE MARKETING MIX

Master the 4 Ps of marketing

Written by Morgane Kubicki
In collaboration with Carmela Milano
Translated by Carly Probert

THE MARKETING MIX

KEY INFORMATION

- **Names:** marketing mix, marketing-mix, marketing mix policy.
- **Uses:** the marketing mix is a basic tool for marketing decisions.
- **Why is it successful?** The model summarises all the tools available to marketers for decision-making.
- **Key words:** product, price, place, promotion, target market.

INTRODUCTION

History

The term 'marketing mix' first appeared in the article entitled 'The Concept of the Marketing Mix' (1948) written by theorist Neil H. Borden (1895-1980), a professor of marketing and advertising at Harvard Business School. He said himself that he was inspired by the research of James W. Culliton (1912-2004) who described the role of marketing managers as 'mixers of ingredients' and proposed a list of twelve elements of the industrial marketing mix at this stage. In 1960, Professor Jerome McCarthy (born in 1928) developed Borden's theory and kept four main points, namely the 4 Ps (product, price, place and promotion) in his book *Basic Marketing: A Managerial Approach*. The mnemonic feature of this approach has contributed to its success and it is widely used by marketers. The marketing mix and the

4 Ps of marketing are often used to express the same idea, although they are not really synonymous. The marketing mix is a concept that describes the steps and choices that companies or brands have to make throughout the process of entering a market with a product or service; whereas the 4 Ps model is probably the best-known way of defining the marketing mix.

Definition of the model

The marketing mix is a marketing concept that includes all of the tools available to marketers to develop efficient actions and achieve their sales penetration targets within a target market.

THEORY

OBJECTIVES OF THE MODEL

The marketing mix includes all of the marketing decisions and actions taken to ensure the success of a product, service or a brand in its market.

The first decisive step in the marketing process: market analysis. Once this is done, the 4 Ps model can be used as a good decision-making tool for marketers. In fact, in addition to covering all of the elements that marketers can focus on, the model is easy to use. Its distinctive name has also undoubtedly added to its success. This classification system is one of the most used in the marketing mix, both in textbooks and in real life.

More broadly, the marketing mix model can be used to help decision-making in the context of a new offer on the market, as well as to test an existing marketing strategy.

CONTEXT AND THEORISTS

The marketing mix appeared at a time when a significant increase in consumption was observed. During the postwar boom (period of strong economic growth between the end of World War II and the first oil crisis, experienced in most developed countries from 1946-1973), there was an explosion of mass consumption. Before that time, marketing was simply used to understand the preferences and behaviour of the consumer; with the arrival of the marketing mix it was then possible to obtain an overall view of the placing of a particular product on the market. Although this theory is attributed to McCarthy, who identified the 4 Ps, he was actually inspired by the list compiled by Neil Borden in 'The Concept of the Marketing Mix'. The professor also admits himself that he was influenced by the research of his partner, James Culliton, who described the role of marketing managers and 'mixers of ingredients'. Later, Philip Kotler (born in 1931), the father of modern marketing, took the 4 Ps concept and offered an updated version in his most famous book entitled *Marketing Management* (in collaboration with Kevin Deller, Delphine Manceau and Bernard Dubois).

The authors did not all agree on the nature of the marketing mix elements. Neil Borden spoke of 'procedures', but today the terms 'parameters', 'tools' or 'instruments' are preferred.

Neil Borden's original list contained 12 elements of the marketing mix that should be taken into account by the marketer:

- product
- price
- branding
- distribution channels
- personal selling (face to face)
- advertising
- promotions
- packaging
- displays
- servicing

- physical handling
- fact finding and analysis.

Meanwhile, McCarthy suggests grouping these variables into four categories, or four levers of action:

- product
- price
- place
- promotion.

The 4 Ps of the marketing mix

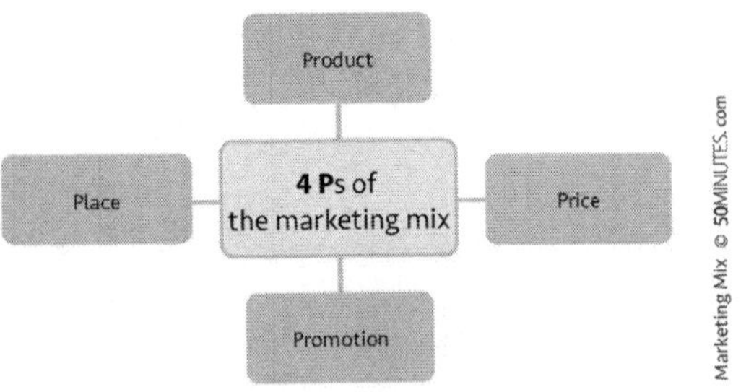

In reality, these lists, whether composed of twelve or four elements, include all the tools available to a company to influence their sales. Nonetheless, this theory has no concrete proof and does not ensure 100% effectiveness in decision-making in any case. The quality of the marketing strategy implemented lies in the relevance and coherence between the four elements that make up the marketing mix theory. In a sense, this can be summarised as follows: the right product, in the right place, at the right price, at the right time. To do this, it is necessary to:

- create a product or service that a particular group of people wants;
- sell it in a place regularly visited by these individuals;
- market it at a price that corresponds to customer expectations;
- make it available when these customers want it.

This approach is appropriate, but one must not overlook the significant workload required to collect all the necessary data, such as needs, expectations and behaviour of customers. It is still necessary to determine how to produce the good or service, at what price and when it should be marketed to optimise sales. This idea requires detailed knowledge of the target market, which is also required. Here, market analysis comes into play.

THE COMPONENTS OF THE MODEL

Product policy

A 'product' is an offer that meets a need in a market. In other words, a product can be a physical object or a service introduced into the market to satisfy the desire or need after purchase and use or consumption. Product policy refers, therefore, to the choice of characteristics for goods or services offered by the company, in other words the nature, quality, size, design, etc. It can also include decisions about the brand, packaging, label or the product range.

Pricing policy

The price is the amount of money the consumer must spend in order to acquire the product. Pricing policy includes the concepts of:

- fixed price, i.e. the price offered in stores
- discounts
- payment terms
- take-back conditions
- credit conditions.

This questions the process of fixing the price of a product or fixing prices within a range. Pricing policy is not fixed and may change depending on promotions or according to the life cycle of the product. It must take into account a number of constraints and variables, among both producers and consumers: cost price, product image, distribution costs, price elasticity (i.e. the impact of a price change on consumer demand), competition conditions (monopoly, oligopoly, competition, etc.).

Distribution policy

The P of 'place' corresponds to the distribution policy.

It involves:

- distribution channels
- distribution networks
- assortment
- locations
- availability

- transport
- logistics.

The company has a duty to establish and maintain the distribution network, and also to choose its sales outlets (its own stores or distributors) that will be responsible for presenting the product, ensuring its shelf availability, offering promotions, or providing advice to customers.

Communication policy

The fourth P, 'promotion', involves communication.

The communication policy mainly includes:

- advertising
- direct marketing or marketing in sales outlets
- public relations
- sponsorship.

Paradoxically it may, to some extent, affect price (premiums, coupons or limited time special offers, for example), but it remains an act of communication and not a pricing policy.

The interdependence of these policies

The marketing team needs to ensure that these decisions are made with thought to distribution intermediaries and end customers, while the marketing manager is responsible for understanding the needs and expectations of customers and providing an offer or solution. He informs customers and chooses a price that is in line with their perceived value of the product. He must then determine the retail outlets in which to distribute the product.

For the four policies, each decision must be made with thought to the target consumers and the positioning that the company has chosen to adopt. Moreover, other areas must be also considered, as if these decisions are made separately they are of no interest. In fact, the strength of the marketing mix is combining all of the elements available to marketers.

The relationship between price and product is essential, but not the most important one. All the marketing mix elements have an influence on the others. For example, pricing must take many variables into account, including the other Ps, i.e. the brand, distribution and the communication network. Promotion or distribution may also influence the selling price. In 1979, Paul Farris and David Reibstein examined the relationships between variables to determine their influence. Thus, a standard quality brand, with a strong advertising backing, can easily increase the price of its products. Distribution also has a fundamental influence on the pricing policy. For example, a company cannot set its prices without knowing whether the product will be distributed directly by the brand or through an intermediary, which may be a small reseller or a large retailer. These choices have an indirect impact on distribution costs, which are a core variable within pricing policy. In short, the variables are interdependent.

LIMITATIONS AND EXTENSIONS

LIMITATIONS AND CRITICISMS

Effective management of the marketing mix will create value for the company in the eyes of its customers. Therefore, the most necessary condition is that of knowing the target and defining the positioning of the brand in the market. Strategic planning consists of managing all of this data with the elements of the marketing mix. Establishing a model using the principles of this theory is not enough if a study of the target market has not already been carried out.

Most critics of the model refer to the 4 Ps, rather than the marketing mix itself. The marketing mix, in its broad definition, consists of the 'operational marketing tools' that allow companies to target their market and achieve the expected benefits (Kotler et al, 2009: 29). It is difficult to really criticise the marketing mix itself; more often, criticism is aimed at the way of approaching it.

The authors who have criticised the 4 Ps typically suggest that this classification system should be improved. Louis Michel Chevalier and Pierre Dubois, in their book on marketing, put forward the idea that the 4 Ps do not reflect the product brand, which is a link between product policy and communication policy. In the model presented by McCarthy and later taken over by Kotler, however, the name of the brand is part of the product policy. Michel Chevalier and Pierre Louis Dubois also claim that although the marketing mix must consider the 4 Ps simultaneously, the different policies addressed are almost never managed by the same person. In fact, the marketing mix model is presented as a whole, which suggests that a single person or team makes all the decisions. However, its components often belong to different sectors of the company. Thus, the product policy may come from a CEO or innovation services, while the communication policy is handled by the communication services.

Lastly, we must be aware that the marketing mix is just a general tool to assist in decision-making. If you look at the details of each policy, there are other, more specific concepts to master. For example, the pricing policy requires more knowledge of concepts such as return rates or perceived value.

RELATED MODELS

The 7 Ps

To make up for the shortcomings of the 4 Ps model, some authors recommend the addition of new components. The best-known of these models is the 7 Ps (1981) by Bernard H. Booms and Mary Jo Bitner, which complements the 4 Ps defined by McCarthy, adding in people, process and physical evidence.

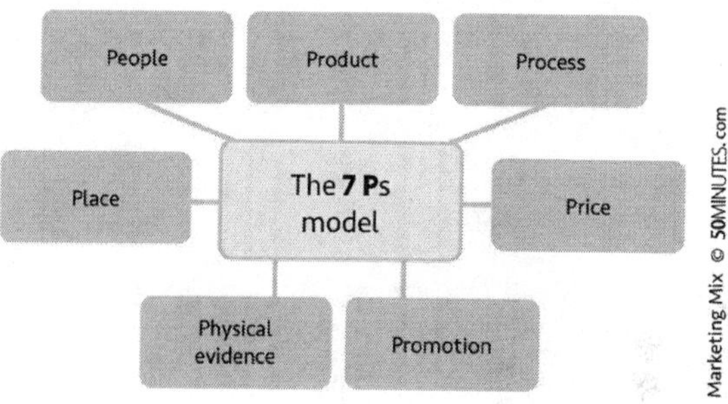

- 'People', as understood by the 7 Ps, do not represent the company's customers, but the staff who implement the marketing strategies. Their influence is important, because they are in contact with prospective customers. The reputation and image of the company are in their hands and seen by their eyes. 'People' are one of the few elements of the marketing mix with which customers can interact.
- 'Process' refers to the way the marketer provides an effective and appropriate customer service. This can include customer service, advice, opening hours or even home delivery. It is a way to build brand loyalty.
- 'Physical evidence' means the physical components of the store, such as the windows or shelf organisation, for tangible products.

We can criticise the conceptual contribution of these three additional Ps, since the ideas they represent can be included in McCarthy's original 4 Ps. 'Process', in the broadest sense, is related to the product concept. 'People' is essentially related to the product and promotion. 'Physical evidence' is understood, at least in part, by promotion.

The S

Other Ps are also proposed:

- Philip Kotler, in *Principles of Marketing* (1986) suggests adding 'political power' and 'public opinion';
- Claudio Vignali and B. J. Davies, in 'The Marketing Mix Redefined and Mapped: Introducing the MIXMAP Model' (1994), meanwhile propose adding an 'S' for 'service'.

The sectors added to the base model also often allow the marketing mix in the service domain to be improved. According to the teachings, this also applies to 'positioning', 'packaging', 'participation' or 'personalisation', that mainly appear in the techniques of web 2.0 and marketing 2.0.

The 4 Cs

A parallel model to the 4 Ps, called the 4 Cs, also emerged to address one of the main criticisms of McCarthy's model, namely the biased perspective towards the marketer to the detriment of the buyer. Robert F. Lauterborn constructed the 4 Cs from the 4 Ps and presented the concept in *New Marketing Litany: Four Ps Passé, C-Words Take Over* (1990): they are focused more on the customer than the product. This model makes sense when you consider that the goal of marketing is to satisfy customer needs.

The 4 Cs are:

- Consumer: product policy becomes the solution offered to the consumer. We must offer customers what they are truly looking for and, to do so, study their buying behaviour.
- Cost: pricing policy is the cost to the consumer. In reality, price is just part of the cost that the customer is willing to pay. Cost includes the purchase price but also the cost of procurement, use and abandonment of a product and the cost of product accessories.
- Communication: this now concerns pure communication, which is more cooperative and tends to create dialogue between the company and the potential customer. The goal is that communication does not only stem from the company, but it also comes from contact with customers.
- Convenience: instead of establishing distribution strategies, the marketer puts himself in the customer's position to understand what the access facilities are to enable them to acquire the product. With the arrival and success of the internet, considering this element has become increasingly important.

PRACTICAL APPLICATION

ADVICE AND TOP TIPS

The marketing mix can help with decision-making as part of a new offer on the market or testing an existing offer. It goes without saying that we must first identify the object to be analysed, whether it is a product, service or brand, for example.

Before building or analysing the marketing strategy based on the 4 Ps or a related model, the company must define its target market. To do this, it must conduct a market study, which will enable it to better understand the expectations of consumers and position themselves accordingly.

Furthermore, it is necessary to perform an internal and external analysis of the company to determine market segmentation (division of the market into homogenous groups of consumers based on their needs, characteristics or behaviours).

The company then follows one or more segments of the market and chooses a marketing target (selected segments according to the strategic interest that they represent for the company).

Once the target has been established, it can define its positioning, i.e. place its product among competitors.

Notice here that the consumers are central to the marketing approach. It is for this reason that the 4 Cs model is often preferred to the 4 Ps, even if the variables here are simply discussed from another angle.

To establish its marketing mix strategy, the company must then answer a series of questions for each component of the model.

Determine the attributes of the product/service

The first step is to determine the attributes of the product or service. To do this, we must ask the following questions:

- What does the consumer expect from the product or service?
- What are the necessary attributes of the product to meet those expectations?
- How and in what context will the customer use the product?
- How does the product look? This question includes the appearance of the product itself, but also its packaging.
- What is the name and branding should be given to the product?
- How is the product different from that of its competitors?
- What is the maximum cost price for its sale to remain profitable?

During this first stage, questions regarding the product are similar to those that must be asked when considering the pricing policy.

Determine the pricing policy

The price can be set according to costs or the perceived value of the product. Whichever approach is chosen, it must be able to answer the following questions:

- What is the value of the product to the consumer?
- Does this product have a base price? Where is it positioned according to its competitors?
- Does the product have much price elasticity? Can prices be lowered to increase market share? On the other hand, would raising the price generate more profits?

Determine the means of communication

With regards to communication, it is not just a matter of choosing an approach. The tools available to marketers are so numerous that a special department devoted to communication is often in charge of finding the best way to reach the target audience, once it has been identified. It is essential to know the target and the desired reaction before establishing a strategy in order to choose the appropriate means of communication. The bulk of spending on communications is devoted to advertising. This can involve campaigns using:

- press (general or specialised)
- displays
- TV
- radio
- cinema
- internet communication.

Remember, even if the sales promotion is linked to the pricing policy (samples, premiums, contests, coupons, etc.), it is still a communication policy action.

We can add to the previous list with other tools, such as:

- public relations
- direct and interactive marketing (using personalisation and interactivity)
- viral marketing (often practiced on the internet)
- selling (which involves an interpersonal exchange between the brand and the customer).

It is also useful to ask the following questions:

- What are the most effective ways of reaching the target audience?
- When is the best time to start promotion? Is the market in which I am operating seasonal?
- What communication activities are used by competitors? Do they influence the choice of actions?

Determine the distribution sites

For 'place', the distribution strategy must be determined in line with the other components of the marketing mix. The positioning of the product/service chosen beforehand inevitably influences the decision on the mode of distribution.

'Promotion' and 'place' also interact if the company chooses to adopt a push strategy (based on the sales force and distribution network) or a pull strategy (based on communication to the consumer and, in particular, advertising) in its distribution policy.

The product itself will also influence the choices: is this a routine or special purchase? Is it a commodity or a luxury item? All the variables defined earlier come into consideration as they themselves are influenced by the distribution policy. For example, developing your own distribution network will influence price and communication. The marketer must still be able to answer a number of questions:

- Where do potential customers go to purchase the product?
- Will customers buy this product more easily in a general store, a specialty store, online or even by post?
- Is the chosen distribution system easily accessible for guests?
- Is managing a sales force necessary?

- What are competitors doing? How can the model be adapted or differentiated?

CASE STUDIES

In this case study, we present two companies that have relied on McCarthy's marketing mix strategy. The first case, dedicated to the German chain store Aldi, is taken from *The Times 100, Business Case Studies* and shows how, in a very competitive industry, a product that is not necessarily innovative can prevail and create value through an efficient strategy of the other elements of the marketing mix.

The second case comes from a conversation between Alain Afflelou, Stephen Gless and Dominique Lichel (*L'Entreprise,* October 2006) and an article by Baptise Diebold (2006). This analysis brings to light the powerful marketing strategy created by Afflelou, which innovates in each area of the marketing mix.

Aldi – creating value through the marketing mix

Since its founding in 1913, Aldi has managed to establish it-self as one of Europe's largest retailers. Its original purpose was to provide customers with products they buy regularly, sold under their own Aldi brand, at competitive prices. In the marketing strategy of this company, the different mar-keting mix elements are all aligned. Innovation is not done through the product, but the way the 4 Ps are structured to create a real marketing mix strategy.

Aldi tries to provide a large variety of standard quality products, sold under their own brand. The first 'P' at the centre of their corporate strategy is 'price'. In order to offer cheaper products than its competitors, the company bases its policy on cost optimisation and adapts the other 'P' policies to suit this goal.

Products are bought in large quantities and little money is spent dressing them up (packaging, brand, etc.).

At the distribution level, the company once again tries to cut costs by limiting the shelving and displays at points of sale. In terms of location of its stores, four criteria are taken into account:

- the number of people who visit or live in the area;
- low competition: Aldi is generally outside of city centres and in places with good visibility from the main road, with minimal surrounding competition;
- accessibility of the store, including via public transport;
- a sufficient number of parking spaces.

The company's communication focuses on customer retention and strengthens the message of price and product policies: Aldi products are of the same quality as those of major brands, but cheaper. Promotional brochures are thus distributed in stores to encourage customers to return. Other than media, the company also focuses on public relations, mailing lists, management of social networks and actions that highlight its products through an external source of the business. To do this, Aldi participates in many annual product competitions. Winning these competitions allows it to increase its visibility, but also its credibility, since a third, neutral party has named their products the best.

Aldi has a detailed sales approach that gives it an edge in a very competitive market. The balance achieved through the marketing mix enables it to offer good quality products at the lowest possible prices. Its communication policy allows it to improve the image of its products while emphasising their prices. Finally, its positioning policy means it doesn't have to increase distribution costs. No major innovation seems to have been made in price, product, place or promotion, but the balance between these four policies has enabled Aldi to find its place in the market.

Afflelou – a success based on innovation in the different elements of the mix

Alain Afflelou opened his first store in 1970 in Bordeaux. By 1984, the chain already had almost 100 franchises. In 2012, the brand had 722 stores across France and more than 1000 in total. This success stems from the fact that the brand managed to innovate in each of the marketing mix areas.

- Product: Afflelou has always offered innovations in glasses and contact lenses with, for example, virtually indestructible glasses. For clients over forty, the brand launched 'Forty', a pack of four glasses that enable them to see up close. These products do not seem revolutionary, yet the brand was the first to offer them.
- Price: Afflelou was the first brand to have proposed bargain price glasses including the 'Chin-Chin' promotion, offering a second pair for an extra euro. The price-product relationship would already have been enough, but

the full marketing mix strategy ensured the company had a truly dominant market position.

- Place: the brand has also innovated in the field of distribution. In fact, it has its own distribution network, but its stores were also the first to have open access frame displays.
- Promotion (communication): the brand allocates a significant portion of its budget to the department in charge of promotion – which is certainly one of the biggest in the sector – and uses sponsorship (partner of the French Open tennis tournament and the Paris Saint-Germain football club).

The Afflelou company has set up an innovative strategy in each element of the marketing mix, while ensuring consistency between them.

Conclusion

The cases of Aldi and Afflelou are very different. For Aldi, the success of the strategy depends on the coherence between the four policies. In the case of Afflelou, success comes from innovating in each area of the marketing mix. Beyond the fact that the marketing mix provides a company with the tools to achieve its goals, the model also pushes marketers to think about their marketing strategy as a whole.

SUMMARY

- The marketing mix provides marketers with a set of tools that will enable it to make decisions in relation to the defined market.
- Objective: the marketing mix is used to launch a new product on the market or to test an existing marketing strategy.
- The 4 Ps: proposed by McCarthy in 1960, this model includes the marketing mix tools in four categories: product, price, place (distribution) and promotion (communication).
- Theorists: Neil Borden introduced the concept of the marketing mix (1948) and McCarthy developed the concept of the 4 Ps (1960).
- Context: the marketing mix emerged in the context of the rise of mass consumption.
- Components: product, price, place, promotion.
- Advantages: the marketing mix neatly summarises all the tools available to marketers for decision-making.
- Limits: the marketing mix is a comprehensive approach to marketing strategy, but other tools need to be employed when working on a strategy in-depth. Decisions concerning the different policies are often the result of several people or services and this makes it difficult to maintain coherence between the 4 Ps.
- Extensions: three Ps are often added (people, process and physical evidence) to complete the four Ps of McCarthy's model. The 4 Cs (consumer, cost, communication, convenience) are another variant of the concept, focusing more

on the customer.

- Tip: before making decisions concerning the 4 Ps, the company must be sure to know the target market in which it wants to position itself.

We want to hear from you!
Leave a comment on your online library
and share your favourite books on social media!

FURTHER READING

BIBLIOGRAPHY

- Alain Afflelou's website:
  http://www.alainafflelou.fr/
- Armstrong, G. and Kotler, P. (2007) *Principes de marke-ting.* [8th edition]. Paris: Pearson Education.
- Booms, B. H. and Bitner, M. J. (1981) Marketing Strategies and Organisation Structure for Service Firms. In Donnelly, J. and George, W. R. *Marketing of Services.* Chicago: American Marketing Association. pp. 47-51.
- Borden, N. H. (1964) The concept of marketing mix. *Journal of Advertising Research.*
- Business Case Studies. (No date) Creating value through the marketing mix, an Aldi case study. *The Times 100 Case Studies.* [Online]. [Accessed 22 May 2014]. Available from: <http://businesscasestudies.co.uk/aldi/creating-value-through-the-marketing-mix/introduction.html#axzz4S2tz9DPH>
- Byrne, K. (2004) Managing your marketing mix. *Chartered Accountants Journal.*
- Chevalier, M. and Dubois, P. L. (2009) *Les 100 mots du marketing.* Paris: PUF.
- Demos. (2012) *Le marketing mix ou mix marketing, de la stratégie à l'opérationnel.* Paris: Demos.
- Diebold, B. (2006) Afflelou entrevoit la vie sans Alain. *Challenges.* Volume 29.
- Faris, P. and Reibstein, D. (1979) How Prices, Expenditures and Profits are Linked. *Harvard Business Review.* [Nov/Dec issue]. pp. 173-184.

- Kotler, P. (1986) *Principles of Marketing*. [3rd edition]. Upper Saddle River (New Jersey): Prentice Hall.
- Kotler, P., Keller, K., Manceau, D. and Dubois, B. (2009) *Marketing Management*. [13th edition]. Paris: Pearson Education.
- Lauterborn, R. F. (1990) New Marketing Litany: Four Ps Passé, C-Words Take Over. *Advertisng Age*. 61(41).
- Magrath, A. J. (1986) When Marketing Services, 4Ps are not Enough. *Business Horizons*. 29(3), pp. 45-50.
- Maillet, T. (2010) *Le Marketing et son histoire ou le Mythe de Sisyphe réinventé*. Paris: Pocket.
- McCarthy, J. E. (1960) *Basic Marketing : A Managerial Approach*. Homewood (Illinois): R.D. Irwin.
- Pariot, Y. (2011) *Les Outils du marketing stratégique et opérationnel*. [2nd edition]. Paris: Eyrolles.
- Van den Bulte, C. and van Waterschoot, W. (1992) The 4 P Classification of the Marketing Mix Revisited. *Journal of Marketing*. pp. 83-93.

IMPROVE YOUR GENERAL KNOWLEDGE

IN A BLINK OF AN EYE !

www.50minutes.com